T0194451

Other books by JJ Campagna:

*For the Love of Me
(Parenting with Intention)
Available now - Balboa Press

Future Books in **The Willow's Bend Series**:

*Journaling and Sifting Through the Fog of
"WIDOWHOOD"
Available Summer of 2019 - Balboa Press

*Sweet Surrender
(Finding Me by the Sea)
Available Fall of 2019 - Balboa Press

Gentle
PASSAGE
ON A WING
AND A PRAYER

JJ CAMPAGNA

BALBOA.
PRESS
A DIVISION OF HAY HOUSE

Copyright © 2019 JJ Campagna.

All rights reserved. No part of this book may be used or reproduced by any means, graphic, electronic, or mechanical, including photocopying, recording, taping or by any information storage retrieval system without the written permission of the author except in the case of brief quotations embodied in critical articles and reviews.

This book is a work of non-fiction. Unless otherwise noted, the author and the publisher make no explicit guarantees as to the accuracy of the information contained in this book and in some cases, names of people and places have been altered to protect their privacy.

Scripture taken from the King James Version of the Bible.

Balboa Press books may be ordered through booksellers or by contacting:

Balboa Press
A Division of Hay House
1663 Liberty Drive
Bloomington, IN 47403
www.balboapress.com
1 (877) 407-4847

Because of the dynamic nature of the Internet, any web addresses or links contained in this book may have changed since publication and may no longer be valid. The views expressed in this work are solely those of the author and do not necessarily reflect the views of the publisher, and the publisher hereby disclaims any responsibility for them.

The author of this book does not dispense medical advice or prescribe the use of any technique as a form of treatment for physical, emotional, or medical problems without the advice of a physician, either directly or indirectly. The intent of the author is only to offer information of a general nature to help you in your quest for emotional and spiritual well-being. In the event you use any of the information in this book for yourself, which is your constitutional right, the author and the publisher assume no responsibility for your actions.

Any people depicted in stock imagery provided by Getty Images are models, and such images are being used for illustrative purposes only. Certain stock imagery © Getty Images.

Print information available on the last page.

ISBN: 978-1-9822-2348-9 (sc)
ISBN: 978-1-9822-2350-2 (e)

Balboa Press rev. date: 04/09/2019

Contents

PART I

How I created a "gentle passage"
and "nurturing shelter" for my loved one.

~ By an enlightened caregiver~

My "faith," my study of new age courses I attended both near and far, have all led me on an incredible journey. It was the information that I drank in for years of study that helped me handle my husband's terminal illness. I am not a "nurse" but a loving wife and caregiver!

What can one do for a loving soulmate who has been diagnosed with a terminal illness?

Answer: Create a "gentle passage" and a "nurturing shelter."
Provide a safe, loving and comfortable place with familiar surroundings, a soft place to fall! My husband and I chose for him to be at home.

A "prepared" caregiver provides "confidence" for the patient, a strong hug when needed and asks for guidance from above, daily! One needs a sense of "direction," has a schedule to follow and if he or she is like me, does it on a "wing and a prayer!" You just do it! You say to yourself, I can do this, I will do this and you do it with "confidence!" Be strong! You become your patient's support system. Prepare, prepare, prepare and "plan" ahead!

My Rooftop Message

I want the world to know that you can make it through a terminal illness with a loved one and come out of it feeling "blessed" and "whole!" I want to share some of my "pearls" as I call them, some "tidbits" that worked for me as a caregiver.

You need a family meeting and put all the cards on the table. Who is willing to do what? There has to be a plan! Even with a plan, for weeks I ran on "automatic pilot." I did the work, but in the background it was others prayers that kept us going. Prayer gave us a "protective coating." I felt as if I was wrapped in layers of "cotton" and "bubble wrap!" It took me many weeks to understand what this feeling was, it was others prayers, cushioning us!

A Purpose to my Writings

I write surely not for fame, but to open doors to teach others there is a way of respecting death, embracing death and developing a course of action to follow if and when a terminal illness is at a loved one's door. Amongst tears can be laughter, smiles, gratitude and appreciation of your loved one's life! If I can do it, anyone can do it, believe me! I could not control the illness, but I could be a "backseat driver" and you can be also, if you choose!

The nurturing love of caregiving is a slice of life that some have never dealt with. Roads of emotion and happiness shall pour over you if you accept this challenge! It is not an easy path, but a much needed one!

My "Prayer"

I surrender all my ego and negativity.
Bless my heart and all who enter through the
pages of this book.
May my writings be a beacon of light
for all who have become lost in illness and
"caretaking."

May my ideas flow with "grace" and "clarity"
and may they be helpful to all who
will attend my lectures or read this book!
May you share these "pearls" of wisdom
with others who are dealing with the terminal
illness of a loved one! May my words help guide
them in some small way.
Amen.

My writings and seminars have given "purpose" to my husband's terminal illness and demise. My writings have started me on my yellow brick road of re-inventing me.

At some point in our lives, we are all given "gray" areas of illness or earthly caretaking duties.

We have free choice to work with the "issues" given us, or we may choose not to! We may run from it, hide from it or turn the duties over to someone else, whom we think may be more capable, "but" before you do, step back and take a different look at the situation! Ask yourself, am I supposed to take the reins here? Am I to "ignore" this and just move on?

I have found that "adversities" given me in life have been solid learning experiences for me!

I have experienced "major" soul growth at the most difficult times of life. Our souls need challenging, they need to grow and expand, otherwise we stagnate!

Sometimes we hit a comfortable zone and we don't want to be knocked out of it! Comfort doesn't always mean good! Comfort doesn't mean your "soul" is growing! No one knows where each individual stands on particular issues!

I once read: Sometimes we have to go out on a limb to reach the "fruit." I found this to be so true.

Caretaking for a loved one, friend, etc. is not "easy!" You may want to scream many times. I would like to teach you to cry gently or "scream" softly! Perhaps take a walk outside or simply blow the whistle (we will talk about a whistle later) when things get tough and believe me, they will get tough!

One person has to take the reins, be the coach, leader, whatever you want to call it. Sometimes those involved in the illness are not all on the same page! At times I found all the doctors were not on the same page with me, at other times, I was not on the same page with them!

Understand you cannot control the illness, but one can learn to be a "backseat driver!"

I once read: You cannot always be the boat, sometimes you have to be the water and just "FLOW!"

Illness has arrived on your doorstep -- where do you go from here? After the initial shock, get your running shoes on, deal with it, this is "life."

Ready, set, go!

Life will never be the same, you will be tested! You need to be prepared! You will need patience and prayer!

Be open, ask for guidance daily! That, my friend, is the "secret tool," asking for God's guidance. It will come!

I kept "negativity" out of our home. I needed all the positive energy I could get, so did my patient. Even if you have to post a sign:

No negativity allowed. Visitors will get the message! No doom and gloom needed!

A sense of humor helped me very much! Learn to "laugh," it doesn't have to be all "sad." Learn from the illness, the adversity, the detour that life has thrown your way!

By creating a sacred space, a "nurturing shelter" for my patient, which is my beloved, is to have his last months of life made "quiet" and "serene!" I don't mean silent, for I had small children in the hospital bed with my patient, reading storybooks, singing music and dancing and marching around my patient's room. I used soft angelic type, fairy type music. We included everyone who chose to visit, to be a part of this journey. My beloved loved life, so we chose not to shut life down! It was a safe comfort zone for the patient, to slowly let go of life amongst those dearest to him! I was "guided" to do this!

Due to the season of my patient's illness, he was able to enjoy the outside covered porch for some lunches and dinner, or just plain fresh air! A change of scenery is always good for the patient as well as the caregiver.

Outside on our patios, within the patient's view, I planted bright colored flower boxes and pots with spring and summer flowers that my patient could see daily through our double glass doors. We were at the seashore where he could see life moving on. Outside as bicycles passed, blue skies stuffed with cotton looking clouds floated overhead!

Of course, if these last weeks were in the winter season, perhaps I would have brought snow inside and have made a basin full of snowballs or perhaps a snowman on our patio wearing my husband's golf hat and gloves! Perhaps even a golf club on his arm instead of a broom.

Remember, I am a decorator, now a caretaker, flying through this illness on a "wing and a prayer!"

A Caretaker's Prayer

One more hurdle, one more river to cross! I know this task is difficult, circumstances so decided, hearts to deal with, much patience, and understanding needed daily!

May my guides and helpers shine forth and blanket us in their bright light. May friends appear ready and willing to serve humanity in a trying way! May my own aches and pains take second seat. May my own heartaches and loneliness be skipped over so I may be a "guiding" angel for another.

Lord help control my mind, my duties, my family and friends. Please send down an abundance of patience and love for this ill person! Wrap he or she like a "babe" in a mother's love, surrounded by warmth and tenderness. May your grace fall upon this sweet soul. May your grace shower down today and every day that follows! Guide us, prepare us, steady us as you have in the past! We shall be your loving servants. Enrich our lives with clarity and understanding. May we teach and set an example for others. Please shed divine light and love on all of us today!

The words I am praying today are so so important! Prayers do not have to be for healing but for "acceptance" of a terminal illness for the patient as well as family members!

May we be a "beacon" in the harbor for the ill person. Shine your light, spread your love for all humanity!

Spoken and Unspoken Words

A "smile" given to someone is an "unspoken" word. A "pat" on the shoulder or back is an unspoken word. Words of encouragement, a compliment is a spoken "blessing."

Some things in life are unfixable. As the old saying goes: The only things for certain are death and taxes! From the minute we are born, it is known that each individual will die at his or her appointed time. People are only loaned to us! Death is not a big surprise! Why are we always shocked (including myself) and startled when one is diagnosed with a serious illness and oncoming departure? If death is inevitable, why are we not better prepared? Why does it catch us so off guard?

Mentally and physically have a plan. Have a routine! Have a backup! Have a caregiver's plan! Line up caregivers if possible. I do realize some have no one to count on! Some may not have the funds to hire help. I understand all this! Hospice and social workers will have answers for you. They will guide you as best they can. I have been blessed with a take charge attitude. I have found if I am prepared 80% of the time,

I can handle any given situation, along with prayers, my angels, and my guides!

Life has thrown me many curves and detours. Divorced at 29, remarried at thirty three, death of my father and other close friends and the death of a beloved spouse, all within a fifteen month period. Mother and I were widows together! All these adversities have taught me something. "Look" and "search" for the lesson, the wisdom in each situation. They are there, it may take time to "discern" them, but they are there!

Reality is: An ill person today has to have an "advocate" that watches out for their health and welfare! It is 2019. Hospitals are different today, care is different today! Be prepared! Private rooms in hospitals are different today! Medicine is different today! Doctors are under different rules! One needs a caregiver or care-watcher 24/7. I personally believe a "terminal" person in a hospital is treated differently than a regular "ill" patient!

Nursing staffs are not all local people, they are brought in from different areas as needed, from different states, towns and other countries. Many older patients have trouble understanding, their hearing is a little "impaired." Sometimes they only hear what they choose to hear! A patient needs someone to "accompany" them on appointments, to understand the medicine changes and new directions!

Who is there really to help? Who is really willing to pitch in? The answer is: very few! This is normal! Try not to be discouraged! This was a learning experience for me!

I have found people handle illness like they handle life, in a "variety" of ways! Some take "charge" and some hide from it! Some like me, pray their way through it! All eight of my adult children handled my beloved's terminal illness differently. It was amazing!

I believe all adversities in life are learning "tools" and we must grasp the "wisdom" from each experience or adversity! A heart wrenching illness that's so devastating may create a huge growth in spirit, soul wise, for the patient as well as the caregiver!

Illness

If you can't fight it, join it. If you can't fix it, accept it and then go on from there! While there is life, there can be joy, you just have to search a little harder! If you enter the illness on a "positive" note you can make this difficult journey a "positive" learning experience! This may sound strange and crazy but I write of nothing that I "haven't" experienced!

As I look back now, as hours, days and weeks passed, I developed a sense of humor. I realized, I alone would help write the script of this sad, sad movie! I would be playing a major part in this "life" drama! I stopped to think, if I were the one "dying," what would I want to see outside my window? How would I want my room setup? Stop and think! Some may not care, it was important to me!

A great "caretaker" is an "angel" in disguise! You may not see the wings, but they are there, they are just invisible right now!

I previously spoke of allowing children in the illness. Teach them to "perform" little acts of kindness, it teaches them they are of value and also teaches them hopefully not to fear illness or death. We had many grandchildren in different states, as well as a small nephew, who when visiting were allowed to dust the room and twirl and dance to beautiful fairy music around the patient's bed (all with my supervision) plus the patient was willing to endure it! Bless his heart!

My personal opinion: The patient may need someone other than his or her mate to confide in. Ask your patient if there is anyone whom he or she would personally want to spend time with, then try and follow through with their wishes!

Remember, they are exiting life. They should have choices if they are "coherent!"

My Tools

I will now write about my personal "tools" of sacred caregiving. The main ingredients of my nurturing shelter include: candles, music, prayer, patience, and a smile.

Items for my Patient

Soft meditative relaxation music, I kept it going from six a.m. til seven p.m. It was calming for me as well as the patient!

I asked for guidance daily!

A sense of humor is a must! Please, please look for the humor in situations, trust me, it helps! It got me through some rough times and broke the tension!

I tried to keep all negativity out of our home as much as possible! I kept "negative" people away from my patient! It is possible!

I personally burned white or ivory candles daily. I found white light helped me as well as the patient! (White battery operated candles can also be purchased.)

A green plant or fresh flowers from my garden, I used daily in my patient's room. I placed one bloom in a tiny vase on my patient's food trays each day.

I also bought funny cards which I placed one a day on the breakfast tray. You may have children make them, it allows them to be part of the illness. The cards gave us a laugh a day!

I rented comedy movies to watch at night. My patient looked forward to watching them!

I used colorful sheets on the rented hospital bed. They seemed to brighten up the room. I chose a soft yellow or green for a man patient. Flowered for a woman patient. They took away the sterile feeling of white, that "hospital feeling."

I used all sizes and shapes of pillows to make my patient comfortable.

Heel pads and elbow pads can be purchased as needed.

I ordered moisture swabs (lemon flavored) for dry mouth and tongue from a local pharmacy.

Large Q-tips sealed type swabs -- individually wrapped.

Chapstick for dry cracked lips was used daily.

Stool softeners - stool suppositories when needed.

I found logging medications very helpful. I had a medication notebook and signed off each medication.

I kept a notebook to log in and out times for aides that I hired. They each added their own care notes on what took place that shift. Example: patient did not eat well, drank nothing today. No output of urine today! Mouth ulcers worse! Keep many pens around! Use "red" pens or pencils to add important information! A notebook is needed for phone numbers and addresses of family, doctors, rental equipment, drugstores, etc.

Things to Discuss with Patient

Important Questions

Now is the time! Discuss now, while the patient can talk, not at the very end of the illness! Some patients would like to help with their own obituaries. Perhaps they have names and dates no one else has. Some, like me, would want to design their own funeral. To some it's a subject to be omitted! Whatever works! My obituary is already written and tucked away until needed! My burial place is ready. Only the date has to be engraved in the marble on our mausoleum. It made my mother uncomfortable, but for us it worked! My husband knew no matter what I did with the rest of my life, he knew my resting place would be near him! He helped me plan and design our mausoleum, he even got to see it! That is a story in itself!

My preparation for my beloved's funeral: As the seasons changed, I had to plan from fall to winter, to spring into summer as to what clothes I would wear for the viewing and funeral (at least I was prepared for all seasons). My husband wanted to wear his "newer" navy pinstripe suit. Some do not care, we did.

Life's Exit

Making Time Count

What does the patient want:

Burial or cremation?

Viewing - yes or no?

Flowers or donations?

Donations to where?

Burial clothes?

Minister, rabbi, priest or none?

Organist, singer, songs and hymns?

Who will the pallbearers be?

Funeral home to be used? Phone number?

Dinner, luncheon or brunch to follow funeral?

Picture board of their life?

Newspaper article written?

Florist to be used? Favorite flower? Favorite colors to be used?

Who will be attending?

Where will out of town guests lodging be?

Asking for Help

Do not be a "caregiver" who is "afraid" to ask for help! "No martyrs needed!" You are "allowed" to have help to wash and dry clothes, fold and put them away! If someone asks, give them a "direct" answer as to what they can do to "HELP." Your patient may still like to read, if not, perhaps someone will read to him or her!

Maybe, you as a caregiver need a long shower or rest. Ask for a "patient sitter" for a couple of hours! The patient may need a professional massage, manicure or pedicure. One may want to give the patient an in house procedure instead of sending flowers. Some whom are expected to help, don't show up, do not despair! This is life! Don't take it personal!

Don't Be Shy

If someone asks you "what can I do?" Have a list:

Rent comedy movies
Drugstore items needed
Grocery items needed
Laundry to be washed or folded
Take out the trash
Prepare a meal or dessert
Drive patient to appointments (local or out of town)
*early stages of the illness
Offer to "patient sit" (to give caregiver a break)

Ask for help. It may come in many ways. Ask for guidance daily, you're going to need it! Do not add to your stress load! Be kind to yourself! No babysitting for others! No errands done for others! No cooking for visitors! You as a caregiver have to set "boundaries!"

Company

How to Deal With It

Most company will call to see if a visit can be tolerated by the patient. At the end of an illness "quiet" may be a must, you decide! What can your patient tolerate, a ten minute visit, a half hour visit? Plan visits around the patient's bath time, meal time, nap time, or evening bedtime. Remember, it's about the patient, not your wants and needs! If company is too much on a bad day, simply say so! How does your patient feel about the visit?

Equipment for my Patient

Items I personally had for my patient (most were rentable):

* Hospital Bed
* Light-weight wheelchair - transfer chair (easy to fold for car, easy for me to lift).
* Commode and cover
* Walker and cane
* 5-position chair/recliner - I rented the first year of illness.
  (later I purchased one.)
* Invacare lift sling (rental) - to transfer patient from bed to chair or commode.

Our home consisted of three different levels. I chose to have small wooden plywood ramps built so I could safely push the wheelchair inside as well as outside.

Clothes for My Patient

After the first emergency surgery on his spine, my beloved needed larger shirts, jackets and coats to fit over his brace that went from his chest to shoulders to bolts in his forehead. Jogging suits were easy on easy off. I used tennis shoes with elastic shoe strings -- easy on, easy off.

Two robes- One winter and one summer lightweight.
P.J.s or nightgowns (combined several sizes).
Slippers
Warm (low cut) socklettes

As the illness progressed and surgeries were performed, I purchased hospital type gowns with velcro. They opened up the back. They are not warm, but easy for changing and could be washed and dried quickly! I used these the last three months of his illness.

Items I Could not Have Done Without

Bendable straws
Bell for patient to ring
Whistle for caregiver to blow, to bring things to a quick "halt".
Baby wipes
Tissues
Bed rails
Q Tips - regular
Lip balm - dry lips
Vaseline
Breath mints
Magnifying glass
Bed pads - washable (2)
Pens, pencils
One red pencil
Room spray
Thermal pitcher and glasses
Paper cups
Mouth swabs (lemon, special order from drugstore)

Notebooks
Address book
Tray with 2 inch lip
Trash cans
Flashlight (small) to use through the night as to not disturb your patient.
Hand towels and washcloths
Two large towels - I chose all white for bleaching purposes
Two sets of twin colored sheets and pillow cases
Mouthwash
Toothbrushes and toothpaste
Soap dish
Denture cleaner and container (if needed)
Diaper pail with lid (to soak soiled items in)
Twin size "thermal" blanket
Twin size spread or afgan for bed
Comb and brush
Razor
Deodorant
Shaving cream
After shave
Hand held mirror
Wash basin
Raised toilet seat
Toilet tissue
Hand soap for aides and company
Body soap for patient

Nail file, nail clippers large and small
Side bed table - rentable to eat or bathe
patient from
Bed pan
Urinal or two
Hospital bed with sides (rentable)
Batteries (for flashlight)
Cordless phone
Candles
Matches
CD player
Station with music on TV (soft meditative)
If patient is at Hospice stage they will order
what patient needs (not clothing or personal
items).

*Please do not "panic" at the sight of my long
lists! These items were gathered over a course
of months into the illness. Some may not be
required at all, for your patient!

Music in the Home

The music I chose to play during the illness kept us all at "ease" as well as the "patient." I believe it let my patient know I was at peace with the situation and in control! Some chants I used during his illness:

"Vision" - Hildigard Von Bungen (Germany)
"Vox Diadema" - Hildigard Von Bungen (Germany)
Benedictine Monks of Santo Domingo - DeSilos
Music for "Guardian Angels"
Reike healing music
Methodist and Catholic hymns
Show Tunes

They were purchased from catalogs. Guardian Angels disc was a gift from his daughter and remains my favorite today!

Stay Calm and Carry On!

If you are calm your patient will feel the same calmness. Keep chaos at a minimum. The "take charge" person must be under control at all times. If you can't be ..... fake it and cry later!

A Variety of Signs for Visitors:

(taped on my front door at various times)

I am up to my "heart" in chaos and work!

Please pray for us!

Accepting phone calls between one and two p.m. only!

Patient is sleeping! Please leave a message in the mailbox or basket below. Thank you.

Patient dreaming, quiet please!

Today is not a good day for visitors! Thank you for being understanding!

No smoking at any time! Thank you.

If you have a cold or not feeling well, please do not visit the patient. Thank you.

My patient had three surgeries in fourteen months before Hospice was called in. Once Hospice took over, they were our support system. They took over as far as supplies needed, medications ordered as well as any needed equipment to be added or deleted! They provided an aide several hours per week "only," the last twelve weeks of the illness. All other hours are provided by you. A social worker and RN checked in once a week. We were able to call Hospice and ask questions as needed. A minister also visited, provided by Hospice, once a week. Their comfort and care were excellent and so appreciated! Special people, providing special care!

As Hospice entered the illness, my white candlelight, music and atmosphere continued! Doctors visits stopped once Hospice took charge!

At the End of an Illness

From my experience, I feel quiet and harmony in the home is "very" essential for the patient. My family was able to control this. I realize sometimes it's not controllable! I realize not everyone understands "noise" keeps the ill patient attached to life. The sights and sounds of the old familiar, frequent questions to the ill, is not letting that terminally ill patient let go! His or her body is shutting down. Life, as he or she knows it, is lessening. "Questioning" your patient may only confuse them! The brain is elsewhere! Their recall is lessening. It's not time for past episodes to be brought out. The patient needs rest and relaxation. It's all he or she can do to breathe in, breathe out. Questions should have been discussed long before this time frame. Let he or she "drift." They have a foot in each world now. They are half here and half there, wherever "there" is in their mind. Noises and different sounds, different voices bring them to confusion, not "peace." They will talk when necessary. They do not need added distractions! Don't confuse "your" wants and need with theirs!

Understand, they are dropping "earthly baggage," little by little! Keep them as comfortable as possible. Do not disturb them any more than needed! Remember, they are trying to reach that "unknowing" path. If possible, someone should guide them with soft music and "direction" not chaos! I used a sound machine or meditation music. Even if they have never meditated, the music is very inviting and relaxing. I have used chants, angel music, zen music, hymns, and reiki healing music.

The patient will lose their appetite. This is normal. Wet their lips with a soft cool cloth. Massage their feet with lotion. Work their hands if they allow, massage may be comforting! "Lock your lips!" Send love and nurturing through your silence. This is not a social time for phone, neighbors, friends, etc. Put up a sign that says "quiet, patient dreaming, sleeping," if needed. Let others talk in another room away from the patient. At this point in the illness, silence is "golden."

These are "my" thoughts and ideas, they worked for our family.

My target audiences are caregivers. I only hope my words will carry them from fatigue and frustration to "hope" and "healing." Life's adversities are "teaching tools" for each individual, for earth is a "school of self discovery!" Once I understood this concept, my "path" became easier to walk! I hope your path becomes easier too!

Grief and sorrow do not last forever! Death of my beloved wounded me, but I walked with it, I befriended it and I have survived and so shall you! This illness taught me so much and started me on my path of "writing."

Some will read my writings and choose to handle illness differently and that of course is their choice! Some circumstances do not allow my way of action.

If one small "suggestion" helps you, I will feel blessed!

PART II

"My Story"

Dedication

I dedicate part II of this book to my guides, my loving family, and my second family of friends who have indeed helped pick me up as I stumbled along my life's journey! I sincerely thank you. I love you all!

Most of all my biggest thank you is to my departed husband, Frank, who encouraged me in life and continues to watch over me. I must bring the essence of a man through the pages of a book, for my grandchildren were too little to remember him. Some, not even being born until after his death. They would have so loved him!

Life had thrown my beloved and I a major detour two months before his retirement. Instead of being carefree and enjoying retirement, cancer now took over our world. I say our world, but it was his journey of pain and courage. I had to become a backseat driver and that I did! I was indeed a take charge person, however, illness and death I was not in charge of!

Follow me on my husband's journey of his terminal illness, from feeling powerless to being prepared. Feel my frustration and fatigue change to acceptance and awareness, followed by action! This all took place by using patience and prayer, working this all together and keeping a sense of humor brought peace to our home, family and situation. It was my husband's journey and eventual demise, but I now realize it was a right of passage for me, an initiation on my own personal journey of writing, an opening up to my creativity, bringing something positive out of a "negative" situation. Who would have thought?

My Intention

I want to serve humanity with the words given me. I want to give hope to individuals who feel hopeless in this chaotic world of today. I would like my journey and my trials to profit others! I want them to know they can make it through the difficult times of a terminal illness.

Inner Strength

It's not your roots, your heritage, your background or your money, it's not your IQ or your education, it is inner strength that's most important! It gets you through life's rough spots, life's trials and tribulations. Lord lead me!

Fatal Diagnosis

This illness hit us head on! My husband's fatal diagnosis, kidney cancer, brought my fairytale world tumbling down! As hours, days and weeks passed, I developed a sense of humor. I realized I alone would help write the "script" of this sad, sad movie. I would be playing a major part in this life drama. I have to do this right! Lord, "lead" me, and that He surely did!

On a Wing and a Prayer

My husband's illness arrived out of the blue! I found I had no time to read books about a terminal illness, it came upon us so fast! I decided to journal my path as wife and caregiver. I was led to guide my beloved's illness with pen in hand! I embraced it, accepted it, dealt with it and prepared for it as best I could. I soon learned a sense of humor was essential. It helped so much! I asked for guidance daily and prayed for patience several times a day. I was "determined" to do this "right." I prayed for acceptance of the illness, especially for the patient and for our family members, knowing there was no cure unless a miracle takes place! A miracle happened, but a different type of miracle.

When it was over, I would write and teach about my experiences, to hopefully help others who were lost in the fog of a loved one's terminal illness. I would write from my soul level as an enlightened caregiver, for I am not a nurse. I worked at our local hospital for four years, two of them in the operating rooms front desk, girl Friday, timing and logging each operation. I continued after marriage working in my husband's medical practice for four years. He, a "gifted" eye surgeon was now the patient!

As I entered the caregiving stage of this illness, I read several books on the subject. They were not getting to the nitty gritty of what I needed! I decided to write my own journey on how I was led to guide, embrace, accept and deal with this detour life had thrown us! I had sense enough to realize there would come a time when I couldn't think straight. Knowing my "detailed personality," I wrote away as to what had to be done right to the end! At this time I did not know of the three surgeries that would take place in a hospital out of state. I had no idea what was in store for us. I guess it's better to simply "adjust" as it comes! I asked for guidance "several" times a day now! I am a realist, I had worked around medicine long enough to know this stage of kidney cancer was terminal!

Reflecting Back

Celebrating my husband's sale of his medical practice and oncoming retirement, we boarded our flight to beautiful Portugal. Seven days into our dream celebration we visited an ancient wine cellar. It seemed to be carved in the side of a mountain with eighteen inch beams holding up its low ceilings. As we were finishing up the tour of this winery, I realized my husband was not directly behind me. I paused for a few minutes for him to catch up. When he did not appear, I retraced my steps and found him standing in a "dazed" state holding his head and neck area. He stated, "Do not touch me. I bumped my head. I know I did damage somewhere!" He said he came up full force and hit the low thick beam! "Just give me my space, I am ok, I just need to regroup myself. Please don't touch me!" I don't even remember telling the tour guide about his accident. My husband did not want to be treated in an "antiquated" hospital in a foreign country. We were seventy two hours from the end of our trip. He felt he would deal with it in the United States. He chose to rest the next day as I packed for home. He was uncomfortable, but still did not complain.

We changed planes twice and as we boarded the bus line in NY airport to head for our final flight, he hollered with each bump we went over. The flight home seemed forever!

After arriving home, we met our local orthopedic physician who checked my husband out and ordered an MRI for the next morning. This was the beginning of my husband's incredible journey which came as a complete surprise to us, for he was incredibly healthy, rarely even a cold, not even a cavity in his mouth. He played golf twice a week and tennis once a week.

Two days later, at seven a.m., the orthopedic physician beat on our front door and said, "Pack a suitcase now, I am shipping you to Philadelphia. The ambulance will be here at nine a.m." Of course we knew this was not good, but did what we were told. I somehow knew to pack also a suitcase for me! I called my friend and neighbor, who came over to our home. She now says it was like a "three ring circus." My husband telling me I was packing too much and me yelling, "I'll handle this! Just lie down!" I guess it was quite funny, me packing for a lengthy stay and him wanting one robe, one set of pajamas, a set of underwear and a toothbrush only! I won, needless to say! The next morning he was in for a six and one half hour surprise surgery! Oncologist, kidney specialist and surgeon greeted us as we entered this first hospital room. It now hit us like a ton of bricks. I knew when he shook my hand and introduced himself as an "Oncologist," my heart sank, now knowing this can't be good!

He spoke of the cancer they discovered and his course of action they had talked over, along with his local personal physician. We didn't have time for shock. I now knew why I had packed a suitcase for me! It may have been a worse shock if we had days to prepare! Angels sometimes work in strange ways! They did additional testing on him through the night and had him ready for surgery at five a.m. sharp. As they put him on the stretcher he said to me, "I will see you in a few hours, take care of the children." His nurses informed us it could be anywhere from a six to ten hour surgery. He now stated to me: "Do you understand how serious this is?" I said, "Yes, I do now!" That is how fast it all happened, I kid you not.

I called my parents and they arrived several hours later and found me walking down the hallways with my suitcase in hand! I had been asked to leave the room I was in! I think that is when I started walking in a "fog." I was in a strange city, with no car, for I rode in the ambulance with my husband. I had no place to stay except an intensive care waiting room. Luckily my parents steered me back to the admissions office for information.

Automatic Pilot

At fifty one, my fairytale world came crashing in! For the next eighteen months and three surgeries later, I was on "automatic pilot." My guardian angels took over for me. I learned very quickly it was up to me and God to get through this. No one was there one hundred percent to help. Everyone had their own lives to deal with. The people that were usually my right arm, namely my father, were not here for me. My dad drove us home from the hospital after my husband's second surgery, tucked him into his rented hospital bed, went home and died suddenly. Life had thrown me a double whammy! I decided right then and there that God must think I have strong shoulders to be given all these tragedies to handle at one time. At the same time, my youngest aunt, only ten years my senior, suffered a major stroke. She was now in a local nursing home unable to walk or talk or even write. She could not speak, but understood everything. My usual helpers, my mother and my angel aunt were busy daily at the nursing home taking care of their baby sister. They were dealing with their own grief, the loss of my father and their sister's illness. They were both widows now. They both knew what was in store for me, me now knowing was a blessing!

How did I survive? Answer: One day at a time, one foot in front of the other! I survived on daily prayers. It got to the point I couldn't pray anymore. As I reviewed my husband's illness and oncoming departure for the first time in my life, I was not in control! The illness was something I couldn't find my way out of. I couldn't take a course and learn how to deal with it and I couldn't depend on friends or family to take over!

Working Through the Fog

Where do I go from here? I cannot change the end result, I can only master today! Prayers kept me going, not my prayers but others praying for my husband and for me. For the first time in my life, I found it hard to pray! I was taught as a child to pray. When I could bring myself to pray it was for guidance, to show me the right way to handle things and the easiest for my husband. I kept thinking, I'm in this alone! No, we are in this together. It is our journey!

I knew my husband's illness could make me or break me. I also knew I wanted him to have a peaceful ending! I had to keep calm and keep my wits about me. At times I felt I was on automatic pilot, existing, functioning, but floating above it all. It was a very strange feeling! As I look back now, I was being "cushioned" by prayer. I had always taken control of everything in my life. If I didn't know how to do something, I would take a course and learn how to do it, or make it or have it done. I was not in control of death. How do I handle this? I can't jump over it, I can't crawl under it, and I can't whiz through it! I realized I couldn't be in the driver seat but I could be a backseat driver and that I was!

We both knew death was inevitable, so we embraced it. We verbally didn't speak about it but we each knew how this would end. All through my life if I needed help with anything I could call up my dad or my mother or my aunts or uncles or grandparents. We have always been there for each other, all living in the same town made it easier. The circumstances now became so "foreign" to me, but thank God, I was able to take the reins and was "guided" through this illness!

Reflecting Back

Out of the Blue

This can't be happening. I'm at the registration desk. I'm here and it's still not registering in my brain. In bold letters I reread again Oncology Department, CANCER CENTER. Oh my God, this can't be happening Warm tears start to flow. I'm not crying. I'm not sad, I'm in "shock" I guess. I feel the warmth of my tears hit my cheeks. I cannot stop them! It's not a normal cry that one can stop. It's as if my very soul was crying! I have never experienced this before. I have now used a half a box of tissues from the registrar's deak. I wiped the tear stained papers off and apologized as I hand her the stack of signed permission slips. I seemed to be fine as they led my husband away in his wheelchair. I was fine again, until I saw the huge sign above the beautiful brick building. We joked as I pushed him down plush Walnut Street in Philadelphia, Pennsylvania, he pointing directions, unable to turn and give them to me verbally.

We moved into an apartment at noon yesterday. Our guardian angels had already intervened and made the apartment available to us.

I miss my Dad whom I just buried. I miss my new grandbabies. I miss my "uncomplicated" but busy life! I miss my secure world. I miss, I miss, I miss. Where do we go from here?

Before Death

I am a realist. I look at things as they are, not what I want or think they should be. I knew this type of cancer meant eventual death. I prepared myself, my home and all eight adult children to have an understanding of what was about to take over our lives! If I am prepared, I seem to be able to handle most things coming my way. Major things I seem to be able to handle, it's the small things that drive me crazy. For example: The cleaners losing my slacks, a lost receipt that I now cannot find, that I put away for safekeeping. Cancer, I considered a major, so I began my list making, items needed, and dove in head first, ready or not, here I come! I can handle this!

Angels on My Shoulder

As I write, warm tears wet my papers; tears that bring back loving memories of the special love affair. I have to think of each individual tear as one of those memories! I grew more from my husband's illness than from any other time in my life. His illness has led me on an unforgettable path, a journey that will be with me forever! I am writing and reliving the past that I walked for eighteen months and now realize I walked the path with two angels on my shoulders, guiding me all the way!

Those angels are still there today. Right now they are pushing me to write my "Willows Bend Series." As I write, I heal. As you read, I only hope my words somehow inspire you to hold on, to grasp and appreciate each experience that's tossed your way. Both the negative and the positive experiences are all learning tools. It may take time for their meaning to unfold and piece together, but eventually if you keep yourself open and stay positive, things will piece together like a mosaic. Then, and only then will you understand!

Description of Angels

Angels come in many forms, not all with feathered wings and harp music. A comforting word from someone, a gentle touch, sometimes just a smile, a friend who calls when you need support or a special friend who gives you that extra push or shove to move you along your path. While you're taking time to look for your angels don't forget to be someone else's angel, that's even more important!

Where do we go From Here?

As my husband's illness continues I feel like I'm living a bad dream! I want to wake up so everything will be alright again, only to realize it's not a dream, it's for real! It hurts, it hurts so badly! I think of the sunshine he has brought into my life and in the children's lives! I think of his wonderful positive attitude and his wonderful smile. I have been so blessed! I am so lucky to have had him as my teacher, my friend, my lover and my guardian angel! What will I do without him? He is such a part of me. I can't remember what it was like without him in my life!

As I reread these printed pages, I'm feeling so blessed; so blessed reading my own writings, an awakening for me, a truth moment! If I can find solace in these pages, perhaps others will too!

Perhaps these writings will help many who are hurting, hurting in different ways! Hurt is something we cannot avoid, no matter how hard we try, it reaches us usually at the most inopportune times. It attaches to everyone. Red, yellow, black or white, rich or poor, hurt happens! How do we begin to deal with this? My only answer is beginning with a prayer, "Lord, guide me today." I ask for your guidance and strength.

Denial

Denial is part of the fear. I don't believe my husband nor I were ever in denial. We knew what the test results meant. We prayed for guidance daily, that's all we could do! We just handled it, which is still amazing to me!

Flowing with the Illness

Healing comes in many forms. We are now personally in shock. We pray for acceptance of this terminal illness as a couple and as a family. We need to learn how to handle and accept the situation, this crossroads on our journey. The bottom has fallen out of our world. I once read: Sometimes you have to be the water and not the boat, and just flow. My husband and I opted to flow! Lord, lead us!

Mastering Today

I cannot change the end result which is death, but I can "master" today. Prayers keep me going!

Upon Awakening

You get up in the morning and you say, "Lord lead me today because there is too much to deal with." You go on "automatic pilot" and you deal with the illness, that's the simple truth, it's all in God's hands!

Dealt Our Hand

Cancer is a part of our family now. It has arrived and has changed our family's entire life. First came shock, then reality set in. How do I deal with this monster? We now have to understand our plight, accepting the hand we've been dealt is another thing. We must teach. We must set an example for our children. We are going to live every second of every day.

If you can't beat it, join it! On a bad day, if possible, stay in bed. Pull the covers up over your head, you're allowed! If needed, cry for ten minutes, allow the sadness, then turn it off and count your blessings!

Our Contract

After we found out my husband had a serious medical problem, I sat down and began to write. I wrote the following as the contract that we two would make with each other: The test results will be coming back soon. They may be good, they may be bad. Whatever they are we cannot allow it to change our life! The results will be dealt with in the following manner: The power of God, the power of prayers and our positive attitude will see us through this! We will not allow any negativity to be in our lives, only positive thoughts. We will be praying for guidance from this day forward and for every waking hour we have together. This positive force will teach our adult children the true meaning of life. We will teach them what a meaningful "marriage" and "partnership" is, in sickness and in health! We have been blessed with eighteen wonderful crazy exciting years! How can we feel cheated? I've been truly blessed to have you a part of my life. Frank, you have taught me what love is. You've been my teacher, my guide, my friend, my provider! What more could one have in one's lifetime? You have loved and accepted my children and grandchildren as your own. You have loved them and appreciated them and are just as proud of them as I am. I won't allow you to be sad. Only smiles are allowed. You will not allow me to be anything but positive and happy, no matter what! I will not allow you to have anything but positive and happy fun thoughts. I will be here for you through thick and thin, you know that.

I love you.
JJ

There was sadness, but we did not allow it to take over and consume us. We worked through it in our own way!

Backseat Driver

I found I had no control over this fatal illness called cancer. For the first time in my life, I took a backseat approach, and guess what? It worked for me. If I can do it, so can you! Since I couldn't be in the driver seat and control this illness, I could be a "backseat driver" and help "direct" the way the illness was handled. This was shown to me several times early on. I knew I could direct my family situations, schedules, etc. I knew my husband and I alone could make this detour of life, this adversity, somehow into a "positive" teaching experience for our eight adult children and many grandchildren!

If we were ever able to set an example, these next twelves to eighteen months was our opportunity! All eyes were on us, family, friends and community My husband had always been blessed with patience and a smile that could light up the world and a positive attitude that helped make the illness doable. He was about to be brought to his knees!

It was amazing how he handled the news. His strong faith and determination was brought into action! For you who are caregivers or family, I would like to share one of my pearls with you: Try to remain positive in the most negative of situations! There are many situations that we certainly could have cried! Instead, we decided to laugh, to laugh at the chaos and craziness that our carefree routine had become!

As I began my journey into enlightenment, some twenty five years ago, I read everything I could get my hands on concerning New Age. I went from one book which would lead to another, to another, to another. I couldn't get enough! I guess it was then I realized, all you take with you is love and knowledge! That's when my true education started. It was also when the teacher in my relaxation class looked at me and said, "Joan you can read and read but at some time you have to walk the walk."

Prayers helped cushion me through his eighteen months of illness and continue today. It all happened. It was and is all very real! It's like

I participated in this drama and now can't believe it all happened!

My mission for those eighteen months was to help my husband pass over the "easiest" way possible with understanding, not fear, with love, not bitterness and to set an example for our children who are now heading households of their own. The way we handled this illness could be a "guide" and take fear out of the death experience.

I realized I was the key player here. How I handle things now was extremely important. I had to be grounded enough to carry this off. I owed this to my beloved. My focus was on him. Again, I couldn't pray for healing. I knew God wasn't going to heal him because he was now in an advanced stage of cancer.

Reflecting Back

Seeing "Cancer Center" again on the outside sign, swept a river of tears through my body that I could not control! I held strong until my husband was out of view, he heading for the radiation department. My tears just kept flowing!

Gentle Passage

We didn't pray for healing. We prayed for "understanding" and "acceptance" of the illness. I prayed most of all for a "gentle passage" for my beloved! As things started coming to a head with the terminal illness, I prayed for focus and guidance. I prayed for strength and all of the above arrived!

Looking Back

I was of little help and comfort to my mother because of my own hurts, the timing was unbelievable! God threw it at me. What could I do but pick up that ball and go with it? I planned Dad's entire funeral and gave the eulogy after the minister finished his. I felt I had to be a pillar of strength for everyone. If I folded, everyone would cave in. I did it as a "tribute" to my dad. He watched me speak at his younger brother's funeral and I wrote a poem about my uncle the night before. I guess that was my first speaking engagement dealing with death. My dad was delighted that I took part in the service. He beamed through his tears, so I had to do no less for him! The strength just came. It also showed my children and stepchildren that there is a positive way to handle life's crises. Be strong!

Embracing the Shadow of Death

We look you "straight" in the eye.
We do not fear you.
We respect you.
We understand your purpose.
We know each individual soul reaches this point
at the designated time.
We thank you for waiting this past year.
We rejoice for each day you're prolonged.
Be gentle with my sweet prince
as you wisk him through the tunnel towards
that bright light.
His years are nearly finished and his works
well done,
but his love for life still exists.
He loves mankind.
I cannot bargain with you.
I know it's inevitable and yet I want to beg
for time
but I cannot be selfish.

He never got to see world peace, this was his dream!

Perhaps his offspring, those beloved grandbabies
will help bring peace to this world, perhaps that is their mission!

Coping

Today I play the role of baker, bather, cook and wife. I realize I am giving of myself like a new mother gives to her child, unconditionally. This is unfamiliar territory! I have not been here for a long time! My children are now adults. Life is now throwing me a curveball. I am encountering a major detour!

Embracing the Illness

My husband's first emergency surgery was to be six to eight hours long. While he was in the operating room I slept in a fetal position. I curled up in one of the medical student's apartments. It was as if I were drugged! I couldn't stay awake. Maybe this was my way of handling the shock of the surgery. We only knew about the surgery six hours ahead of time. The rug had been pulled out from under us. Our world was in complete chaos! My parents arrived and stayed with me during the surgery. They ran back and forth between the family waiting area and the apartment I was in, down the street.

Surgery Number One

My parents were my lifelines. They couldn't understand what was wrong with me! I'm always a take charge person with lists in hand! To find me sleeping through this entire first surgery was totally "puzzling" to them. They brought me my favorite sandwich and drink. I couldn't wake up enough to eat it. They took turns coming in to check on me.

They both arrived later in the day announcing my husband was in the ICU and I was allowed in for a few minutes. "By the way, some tall guy in a cowboy hat stopped by to see you. He asked for you and we told him you were at the apartment. He said for me to tell you it was important to remember the two "huge angels" that sit on your shoulders." I sat up with that comment and became totally awake. I laughed at the description of the large cowboy hat. I knew who it was and understood the message. It was a stranger we had met several days before, working on a missing child case. He lived in the Philadelphia area and was a volunteer on the case. While heading to the hospital I called him and said what hospital we were heading for and had to cancel another appointment we had with him to work on the case. He followed up and came to sit with me in the waiting room in case I needed anything. (Angel in our midst comes to mind.) He was the second person to tell me about the "huge" angels I have around me and I truly am a believer!

Strong Shoulders

I once read a line in a poem, "Into each life some rain must fall." I now add to that, the "adversities that appear in our lives are merely stepping stones." I have found they make me a stronger individual. God must think I have very strong shoulders!

The Villain

At times the medicine seems to be the "villain" instead of the cure! Some days you may both feel like pulling the covers up over your head and sleeping away the stress and guess what, you're allowed! Routines will seem a little insignificant when you're dealing with an illness! If you like eating your dessert first and the meal later, it's your call!

Our Conversation

One year before the death. Talking with my daughter on the subject of motherhood and bonding with her new son, I realized life comes and goes like the tide, in and out, in and out!

I only allow myself to cry when I'm alone. I'm crying for me. I'm crying for my Mom, a recent widow. I'm crying for motherhood. I was crying for everything and everybody. I just wanted to cry and cry and cry! Thank God crying is a release for me. I cry at night when I'm alone upstairs, in my bedroom hideaway. I cry in the car while driving. I have turned the radio off now, for sad romantic favorites seem to throw me over the edge! I find silence is golden! I wonder how long music will have to be kept silent? The "unknowing" is a place I find uncomfortable!

Always Prepared

A navy dress for all seasons. Each season in the last year of his life, I ordered a navy dress suit. I thought I did it without his noticing. When the last one arrived for the spring-summer look, he smiled and said, "Nice funeral dress." We said nothing more and just hugged!

Coping

I just kept dancing life's dance, faster, faster, faster. I was coping. It was working. We were "surviving" and that's all that mattered! I was keeping it all together, day by day. Many friends didn't come around. I found this strange! Many family members didn't show up. I soon realized I was basically in this alone. I learned very quickly that everyone accepts illness and death "differently." Where were my rescuers? Don't they see me drowning? I need help! I had to sink or swim! For my loved one's sake, I chose to swim!

Actress

I feel like I am an actress on the stage. I have a part to play, to portray and I had to play my role and move on to the next act. Problems and situations constantly popped up daily, no matter how prepared I thought I was! I now know friends and family were praying for me through this part of the journey.

Autopilot

I appeared to be so, so busy. As long as I kept moving I didn't have time to stop and "reflect" what was really happening to my own personal world! I was not really grieving my dad's sudden death. I seem to be on automatic pilot! It allowed me to give continuing care for my terminally ill mate. Perhaps God threw me many things at once so I wouldn't have time to fall apart!

Embracing the Illness

I didn't pray for healing, I prayed for acceptance and the gentle passing for my beloved. The right nurse's aides, our angels, arrived and stayed with us to the end. They administered care with love and knowledge, empathy and tenderness. They were a true blessing!

The Gift

The love we share is a gift. I have a heavy load to bear now, but I will carry it reminding myself whenever I need to, that "nothing lasts forever!" I will do my best until the end of his illness. I need to remember the dependable, faithful and loving husband he is. He always sees good in everyone. He always looks at the glass half filled, never half empty! He is always cheerful and smiling, very seldom down or sad. He loved life and never expects anything from anyone. He gave his children and step children roots and wings. Roots of family, love and understanding, and wings to let them fly! He is accepting death as he does life, with "dignity" and "honor." He is the bravest man I have ever known. He never once has asked "Why, why me?" He has never felt cheated of anything. He is so grateful for any little scrap of time anyone gives him. He was so appreciative of the care and faithfulness I gave him. He thanks me daily. He wanted to take care of me and I have ended up taking care of him, that bothers him! He never wanted me to be alone in life. I'll never be alone, for his love and spirit will always be around me! The relationship we two have is emotional, spiritual and physical. Many seldom find that in a partner. We are lucky!

During the last two weeks of the illness a few friends were in and out of our home. One friend pulled me aside and asked me if I realized how many times a day he told me that he loved me? Looking back on it, I started counting. It was amazing and so, so sweet!

How Did I Get Through my Grief?

Two large angels sit on my shoulder, my angels, my friends and my family helped pull me through this rough time. At times I felt like Humpty Dumpty, who had a great fall ... breakable! My faith, my spirituality, positive attitude and sense of humor held me together. I was determined to do this right!

Where Have I Been?

Clearing the cobwebs away! I took a walk down the main street of our hometown with a friend. The air felt crisp, cool. It was great to just be out and about and away from the illness for just a few hours. It felt like I was being let out of a time capsule. Businesses that once were there had closed, some buildings torn down. For a Saturday afternoon, it was extremely quiet. I had not realized a lot of our downtown stores had relocated to the new mall.

The people I did see, I did not recognize! Changes everywhere! Where had I been these last few months? Everything is so so different. I suddenly realized I had changed too!

Experiencing my husband's illness and the acceptance of it, has changed me! Today made me realize, I am truly walking in the "fog" of my beloved's illness.

Reflections of the Illness

Pushing my husband's wheelchair reminded me of pushing my babies stroller, not a burden, but a pleasure. I'm doing something for him, my wonderful, faithful husband! Now I tuck him in at night just like a new mother tucks in her baby. His nightmares are of cancer, the big "C" word! He dreams of cancer cells. I pray his nightmares are few!

Accepting Prayer

When you feel like you're wrapped in a bale of cotton, surrender the feeling, for you're being wrapped and surrounded by others prayers and love.

In the Palm of His Hand

God held us in the palm of his hand these last eighteen months. He sent many guardian angels along the way! They gave us "strength and guidance" and helped keep us on the right path of this surprise illness.

My Morning Message

I Awoke to: My husband was a dying man filled with life! How true this statement is. Some people walk around with one foot in the grave. They are half deceased already. Wouldn't it be wonderful if we could all live every minute of every day? The choice is made by each individual. What do you choose?

What I Have Come to Know

My husband's illness and impending departure brought me to my own soul's "evaluation" of my life! While evaluating my life I found my passion was writing and teaching! What's your passion? Have you found it yet? If not, why not?

Before Hospice

The next several months my husband had three surgeries in an out of state hospital. I had to get my running shoes on, for there were radiation appointments, chemo appointments, out of state doctors appointments with kidney specialists, kidney surgeon, orthopedic doctor and brace fittings. It seemed endless!

After the third surgery we realized, ok we now need to call in Hospice! It's now time. The last three months of his life Hospice was our lifeline! I basically had our home "hospital" room all ready when Hospice arrived. They of course added additional equipment and took charge of most supplies needed as well as medications.

A new form of caretaking was now engaged! My prayers for strength and guidance continued! Hospice arrived, they were our saving grace!

Reflecting Back

Angels All Around Us

During my husband's surgeries, I found "angels" all along my way! An angel security guard walked me safely to my apartment at night, an understanding "angel" surgeon! An angel nurse in ICU who integrated family and patient spirituality! An angel friend arriving from North Carolina slept with me for three nights in ICU waiting room, each of us using two chairs each to make a bed! Even the tech giving the breathing treatments was an angel, with encouraging words! It was amazing! Look for your angels. If you don't feel you have one, ask for one!

Waiting room encounters -- Another patient's family member came up to me and stated: Your family has been such an inspiration for me! It was such a compliment for my family as well as me! One woman asked me to visit her father's room, which I did! She introduced me to her husband and said this was the "glowing lady" I told you about! She's an angel. I answered, "Who me?" I believe as you gather you must give! Be an angel for someone else. Perhaps I was for this lady and her father! I now realize anything is possible!

What do I pray for, thy will be done. I pray for helping hands, the right nurses and aides to arrive, and they did! I am very thankful today for the strangers that provided forty some pints of blood that saved my husband's life as he bled out! I am happy for the most "spiritual" Easter in my beloved's hospital room today. I am thankful for the apartment that became available again today! After the third surgery, months later driving home for additional clothes, I am thankful for the angel "John Boy" as I called him, for stopping me on the Parkway and telling me my car was on fire! My angel out of nowhere drove my friend and I to my home forty five miles away. It turned out he lived twenty five minutes from my home! Wow! Angels certainly watched out for me!

Meditation Disc

Meet your guide, your angel on the mountain top. After I worked the special meditation disc with my beloved, he wrote me, you're my angel at the top of the mountain! (It was an honor for me and brought tears to my eyes!)

He asked for this meditation disc to be played many times during his illness. It relaxed him. One of his nurses made the CD. She eventually left Hospice and I hired her for several hours to do guided meditation work, which my husband so enjoyed!

Silent Tears

I am convinced I am cushioned by prayer. I still am able to laugh in between the silent tears. Silent, because I don't want to upset our adult children. They are dealing with a new phase or new chapter of life. I believe they realize just how special a man their father and stepfather is. His "gentleness" is his "strength." His goodness carries on into each of us. When you love so deeply, how do you detach?

My entire world is changing! I knew nineteen and a half years ago as I took my wedding vows that I was marrying an older man that I loved. I knew someday his demise would most likely be before mine, but it didn't matter. I was in love and all was right with the world. Little did I know that we would be so deeply ingrained soul wise, that we both felt joined at the hip. He thinks and I feel. I feel and he thinks. I will never again in my life let another be such a part of me. I will never have such sunshine that he has provided for me, such warmth, love and completeness.

When my first grandchild arrived I felt complete, like my being was whole. I cannot explain it. Now death wants to take a part of me away and I have to be willing to let go, letting go but still wishing it's a bad dream!

I'm not afraid, I just hurt! I have to detach for his sake. I cannot hold him earthbound. He needs to move on and conquer other worlds or perhaps return again to this world and maybe then experience world peace or help establish it, that was his dream!

Perhaps we will be together again. We have talked of that. I feel we have been together many times, that is why our relationship is so strong! Death will never take that away! We will always be together in our hearts. He has taught me so much! I wonder if he realizes that?

I know my purpose is to make his "transition" as easy for him as possible. I have to guide him to that place with love and gentleness, yet awareness. I have to relax him and let him leave swiftly, but peacefully! I must not cling. I must not vary! My task has been shown to me. My part is not easy, but he has taught me to have courage and strength.

Angel Out of Nowhere

Reflecting Back

During the hospital stay, a group of medical students was led into my husband's room. They had studied his case and stayed for nearly half an hour asking him questions about the illness. Frank, being a surgeon himself, took time and enjoyed their different personalities and answered numerous questions. They parted with a sermon from him, as he always seemed to give everyone! One female doctor stood out above the rest. She seemed to have a "sparkle" about her. I was instantly drawn to her and I couldn't figure out why.

Days passed and the third surgery was performed. Things did not go well, he bled out! Frank was given forty three pints of blood. They couldn't get him to clot and he nearly died that night.

As I got off the elevator from returning from the cafe' I noticed the woman doctor from the week before. She asked how my husband was doing and I told her. She could tell I was upset and took me aside. She sat with me in the waiting room for some length of time. She told me how she herself had had cancer years before and how with each intravenous drip she chanted a prayer and said it was universal and thought it might help us. She left me feeling very uplifted. I am most appreciative of the time she gave me and I prayed her prayer for many months. She was an angel for me!

I visited the small hospital chapel daily and throughout the days chanted this universal prayer. It will always remain very special to me!

Asking

Ask for "guidance" and it will come. Ask for "strength and it will come! I asked for patience and it arrived. I asked for the right nurses to come and they arrived! I prayed for "acceptance," and it came! "Accepting" his fatal illness was being very "brave!" He will always be my "HERO." By my husband accepting his illness, it made it easier for "all" family members to accept.

I know I have two "large" angels that sit on my shoulders and "never" leave my side. They are still with me today!

Dignity

My husband accepted everything thrown his way with "dignity" as he had always handled anything in life. He must have been scared but he never showed it to me! He respected his physicians and did everything he was told.

We learned to laugh instead of cry together. Our positive attitude and prayers made life bearable for the next fifteen months. This time frame was one of the largest growth periods for my soul. The illness taught me so much!

I miss my husband's hugs and squeezes. I miss his strong arms wrapped around me. Lord, make me strong. Lord, help me, help him. Lord, give us strength. We are in this together. He loved life and was willing to try anything to prolong it! After the three surgeries, he changed his mind!

A Purpose to My Writings

I am writing, certainly not for money, surely not for fame, but to open doors to teach others there is a way of "respecting" death, "embracing" death, perhaps developing a course of action to follow if and when death is at a loved one's door! Amongst the tears can be laughter, smiles, thankfulness and appreciation of your loved one's life! If I can do it, anyone can! Believe me! I was a backseat driver and you can be too.

Creating a Nurturing Shelter

My nurturing shelter was now in place. A comfort zone for my beloved! I now had to add the ingredients of peace and tranquility, light and love, realizing this had to begin with me! "Lord lead me" was my prayer daily and it worked! Music softly played from six a.m. to seven p.m. daily! Candles, candles, everywhere, some placed as you entered our foyer, on a console in front of the mirror, this doubled the candle light. Our downstairs was full of peace, comfort and caring! The fragrance of vanilla and lavender was quite apparent as one opened the doors to our home, our nurturing shelter!

My husband being Catholic loved the oil painting my friend gave us from an estate sale. It was of Mary with the sacred heart painted in the picture. As Monsignor visited my patient, he stated, "Let me die like this, when it's my time!" My husband and I smiled, we wanted to high five it, but we didn't. It let me know I was doing it right, right for us and our family! Maybe not another's choice, but very "right" for us! It all came so natural. It all seemed to at last "flow" into place.

After eight weeks in our dark painted library, I needed light and air! It's now late spring. With a lot of thought and prayers I gathered up the supplies of our nurturing shelter and had everything transported to our seashore home, one hour away! The home we were in was set back from the street and life seemed to be passing us by. Moving to the shore, we could see life existing, through our double doors, children passing by on our sidewalks, heading down to the ocean with buckets and shovels in hand. Bicycles passing by in all colors, shapes and sizes! The sunshine was pouring in our windows and pushing our "sadness" to the sidelines!

My world became a conglomeration of candles, medication charts, shift changes and medical equipment. I was putting together a jigsaw puzzle of tools and techniques. These tools were not found in a hardware store, but tools of patience, attitude and organization! My main tool was prayer!

Music throughout our home was so important for my patient as well as myself. Through the weeks and months to come, others told us how relaxed it made them feel! I laughed with my husband several times a day by placing funny cards on his meal trays. I prayed for guidance and cried softly by myself at night! Thank God for friends that were my nightly sounding board!

There were still checks to write, bills to pay, errands to run and appointments to schedule. I still had to keep a home running as smooth as possible and deal with my husband's illness. I didn't have time to be scattered. I had to remain focused. I made it through my beloved's illness because of divine grace. It was showered upon me.

I just kept putting one foot in front of the other. I later realized again, it was other's prayers that was carrying us through! I tried to stand in my faith and my values. I am writing today while sitting in a hospital waiting room. I am writing in hopes that my words may encourage other caretakers that they can do it! In the end cry, but cry for joy that "you" participated in one's hopefully gentle passage!

Home Health Aides

The home health aides I hired administered care with love, knowledge, empathy and tenderness! They were well prepared. They were our "angels unaware!"

Morning Message

I awoke early this morning to the words being spoken in my ear, "God is the sweetness you take of life's challenges." This message is one of my favorites! I want to needlepoint this message on a pillow someday.

Lights, Camera, Action!

The Hospice nurse would save our home for the last visit of the day. I finally asked why are we always last on your list of patients? The nurse commented, "When I walk through your doors, it's like walking into heaven! The soft music is always playing. White candles are always lit throughout the house. The entire home is warmed by your positive attitudes. It glows! Your husband always teaches me something. I always leave here with more than I came in with!" The social worker who checked in on us once a week looked forward to being with my husband. She said she enjoyed him so and that if she could film this home, this atmosphere, it would be a million dollar commercial for Hospice! That thought brightened my day! Her comments let me know I was doing something right!

At that point, I was running on "automatic pilot." I tried to create an atmosphere that if I were in a terminal illness situation what would make me comfortable? Fresh air, fresh flowers and plants, positive attitudes around me, healing music and chants, white candles lit everywhere! I would weekly make a candle and food run. I would light them as soon as my feet hit the floor at six a.m. The music started as I prepared his breakfast tray.

Some friends would come and go, some would sit on the bed with him. I allowed the grandchildren to hop up in the bed with him. He allowed and loved the togetherness! I did not want them to fear illness.

Realization

Prayers helped cushion me through and continue today! It all happened, it was and is all very "real!" It's like I participated in this drama and now can't believe it all happened!

Reflecting Back

As they gave Frank anesthesia, I swear it was like I was breathing it in. I laid on a bed in a fetal position and couldn't function again until I was told he was in ICU and I could now visit him. With that, I was up and at it, full of spirit! It took me many days to realize what had happened! In my heart, we are so connected, I would swear I took on his anesthesia! It was like I was drugged. I couldn't keep awake!

Mastering Today

I cannot change the end result which is death, but I can "master" today! Prayers kept me going! I feel as if I'm alone. Where do I go from here, Lord? This illness of my beloved can either make me or break me! I so want him to have a peaceful ending!

Everyone I could always count on, cannot be here for me now. My mother, a recent widow is grieving herself, trying to pull herself up from my father's death.

My cousin who helped as a housekeeper during this time frame decides she can't stay and watch this happen! She's already in her early life buried two babies. Later in life, buried her first and second husband. I couldn't cave in, I needed to stay in control! My husband needs me more now than ever. I can do this Lord, if you stay with me!

I know the right aides and Hospice workers will arrive! Help did arrive and our move to our shore home went smoothly! My cousin arrived back after five days away. She just needed a break! Thank you Emma, you're an "angel" unaware!

No Regrets

God sent many guardian angels along the way! They gave us strength and guidance and helped keep us on the right path of this "surprise" illness.

I am writing today in hopes that my writings may encourage another caretaker that they can do it! In the end cry, but cry for joy and have no regrets!

Life Changes

My home is changing to fit the needs of my beloved's illness. Wants and needs have changed, life has totally changed. I have changed!

What I Didn't Expect

People disappeared from our lives but new angels appeared! Close couples in our lives did not visit! They sent in a beautiful lunch or card, but didn't visit! I felt like they did not want to be around death. Some visited but did not show for the funeral, this bothered me! This was something that I didn't expect! A real learning process, that I was not in control of other people and how they handle a terminal illness or death!

Windchimes

I did not have time to shop for an anniversary card, so I wrote this story. I wrote it as a child's story, telling the love of their grandparents! I am hoping my grandchildren will read it someday to their children:

Once upon a time, in the kingdom by the sea lived two very lucky people who were very much in love. Their love was so real that it tingled. Their love was warm and fuzzy like an old slipper, a love that each could count on forever and ever; lifetime after lifetime, never-ending just new beginnings. As the legend goes, they taught their little fairies that every time they heard a wind chime tingle they were reminded of the king and queen's love. How they love each other and how much they love their little fairies. They taught them to feel the tingling. They taught them that the twinkling stars were disguised as kisses being sent to all the little fairies. All they had to do to feel the love was look above and receive their kisses as the stars twinkled. They taught them to listen for the wind chimes.

Do you know who the little fairies are in the story:
Answer: the grandchildren.
Do you know who the king is?
Answer: Pop-pop.
Do you know who the queen is?
Answer: JJ.
Who has the play castle?
Answer: JJ and Pop-pop.
Who loves you very much?
Answer: JJ and Pop-pop.

My husband loved this story I wrote as an anniversary card! We had a large castle made of heavy plastic put together in our downstairs recreation area. All the grandchildren played and climbed on it on their visits!

Sharing One's Illness
with Children

They played with his cane. They climbed on his wheelchair. They helped dust my beloved's room (our den). We read stories in his hospital bed in our home. They tucked him in bed, they caressed him with wet sloppy kisses all over his face and forehead and neck. Grandchildren, and a nephew, danced around his bed to angel music, as I called it. He never complained. He allowed it and I think he appreciated their presence! He was arriving at death's door, he had come full circle. He wanted to let the children share in his journey, this last journey, a completeness to this lifetime. I thank him for sharing that!

Dancing Sunbeams

Dancing and twirling with my grandchildren around my beloved's hospital bed was a memory I shall never forget! I was teaching them at an early age that death or illness one should not fear! Joy and love can abide in each situation. One can help his or her loved one to move on with one's journey without FEAR. I am quite sure my beloved left this earth with memories of dancing sunbeams, white candles burning, hearing soft music playing and negativity be gone! Only love was surrounding him! Thank you God, angels and guides, I thank all my helpers. Thank you! Thank you! I wish everyone could leave this earth with this experience and my beloved's faith!

Loving Life

God gave my husband a talent with his hands. He has helped heal thousands of eyes. He also gave him talent with his words that have taught love and given many strength. He lived and loved every day given him. He has found "joy" in each new morning. He has lived long enough to know the joy of grandchildren and to hear the words "pop-pop loves me."

The above paragraph can be a testimony for everyone. Don't wait, start today. Enjoy your life! Love your life! Only love survives. Tell your loved ones today how much they mean to you!

Until the End

The most pleasant memories can be at the end of an illness. It's okay to leave. Give your loved one permission to leave. It's okay! I overheard my grandfather's Chinese doctor say to him, "Harry, it's like getting on a bus, one of us has to get on first, it's okay!" I thank you Dr. James Wong Sr. I shall never forget your gentleness and your words of wisdom! I was a young mother when my grandfather was passing, but I will never forget the message!

May you now also rest in peace.

Loud and Clear

The night before my beloved's passing my gifted friend, Donna, called and said she was receiving the following message from my husband who was now not talking. It was arriving loud and clear. "We were not to rush his passing." It was "coming," but not tonight! As the angels sing into the night, I will follow them, but not until the morning's light.

My beloved passed the next morning at ten-fifteen a.m., only after his daughter arrived from a midnight flight from California. My daughter and sister-in-law and myself were "mentally" trying to help him pass, perhaps too aggressively. He knew our intentions were good. I can never thank them enough for their support and love.

Souls Sweet Presence

I go as far as I can with you, my beloved! I am not permitted to go beyond death's door. I leave you here in the outstretched arms of God.

I thank Him for a friend and faithful loving husband. Your pain is now over and your new journey begins! My mind is filled and overflowing with the "I love you's" we gave each other daily! We needed to say no more!

A hand to hold, that is no more,
except for precious memories in my heart.
No tears to shed for there are no regrets,
just memories of days gone by.
Farewell sweet husband of mine.
The "angels" now await you.
Go dear and don't look back!
Your job's well done, sweet husband of mine!

Sheer Mist

At midnight I knew death was knocking at the door. It was now time. I thought, possibly I could be holding him here instead of letting him go on! I was in my nightgown; I quietly opened my front door and walked down the silent street. I walked eight houses down to the beach where the bay and ocean meet. Not a soul was around, no one missed me, no one even knew I was walking to the beach! In the moonlight I could see way in the distance, a large ship. It reminded me of the poem on the back of a booklet printed by "Hospice."

Gone From My Sight

I am standing upon the seashore.
A ship at my side spreads her white sails
to the morning breeze and starts for the blue
ocean.
She is an object of beauty and strength.
I stand and watch her until at length
she lands like a speak of white cloud
just where the sea and sky come
to mingle with each other.
Then someone at my side says:
"There, she is gone!"
"Gone where?"
Gone from my sight. That is all.
She is just as large in the mast and hull and spar
as she was when she left my side
and she is just as able to bear her load of living
freight
to her destined port.
Her diminished size is in me, not in her.
And just at the moment when someone at my
side says,

"There, she is gone!"
The other eyes watching her coming
and other voices ready to take up the glad shout:
"Here she comes!"
And that is dying.

~by Henry Van Dyke
A 19th century clergyman,
Educator, poet and religious writer

Safe Journey

When my beloved passed, I did not see his soul leave his body, as much as I tried. My sister-in-law and my daughter did! They expressed it was a "sheer mist" leaving the body. We high-fived each other! We did it! We stayed to the end! We helped him pass over! With love and prayers surrounding him, with white candles glowing and soft music playing, my beloved "exited" this earth plane with a piece of each of our hearts! Sunbeams danced through the windowpanes as we, his loved ones, "high fived" each other with tears of joy staining our cheeks. We succeeded our mission! We helped our beloved to pass over as calmly and lovingly as possible! We thank you for being a part of our lives. "Safe journey!"

Heaven Bound

It may sound crazy but I sent someone in the kitchen to fetch champagne glasses and a tray I had set up and the bottle of Dom Perignon given to him last Christmas. We toasted my beloved on his new journey, "Heaven Bound!" He was so ready and we were happy that his pain was over. I have no regrets. I did it "my way" (which was his favorite song). If it worked for us, perhaps it will work for others! For this reason, I must write and share my experiences!

Reflecting Back

Two days before his departure my husband stated: Death is only a "tool" that lets you twist things the way you want them.

~Dr. F.N. Campagna~

Peace

My beloved passed so peacefully, viewing a beautiful potted garden placed around a yard statue of St. Anthony, patron saint of children, patron saint of things lost.

Acceptance

Not everyone may be open and accepting of death as I am. I may come up against people that will not let go and have much fear. For those people we should pray for acceptance; their acceptance of the illness as well as their loved one's acceptance. My husband's oncoming death was accepted by him as well as his loved ones. The acceptance made the situation a lot easier!

My Beloved's Gentleness

I realized my husband was gentle every day and shared his knowledge and wisdom with all of us! Each and every soul he taught love! He loved people and people loved him! Some patients are not "gentle" or kind and are asking, "Why me?" Some have no faith, no peace in their heart and no loved ones around. He personally had taken the time to get all his things in order. He was lucky to have the time and so were we! For that I am so thankful. I know for sure, my entire family made a positive out of the negative situation. He was prepared. He had his "faith" to turn to. He passed with "love," "peace," and "graceful" wit!

Metamorphous

The butterfly shall be significant in my life. It brings forth the following words to mind:

Flying free
New life
New roads to conquer
New adventure
New ideas forming
New truths coming
New paths to walk
New open mind
Awareness

As my beloved passed over, I looked outside the window. There were white butterflies everywhere I looked. My small backyard garden was covered with these beautiful white creatures! I called my daughter to come quickly, I wanted her to share in this beautiful rare moment in time!

The Unexpected Visitor

Grief and sadness have touched our homes and our hearts this week. The unexpected visitor, death, has visited but it shall not destroy those remaining. We are family. We are united in faith. We are strong and though we may not understand the whys, we shall give each other strength and courage. As adults, may we set an example for offspring to be there in time of need and encouragement. For death is the time for mending fences and patching up parts. A healing time. A time of acceptance and moving on with grace. It is a stepping stone of life that we all will reach someday. Let us all "unite" and set a true example of what "family" is and what true friendship means.

Into the Garden

An Angel touched my shoulder
guiding me in my flight
into the peaceful garden
bringing me to the light.

Now it's time for my journey
the light is shining so bright
the bridge I have crossed over
I walk now in the light.

Written by my friend Donna. She wrote this
the night before my husband's passing. I used
this poem at his funeral mass. May you also
rest in peace now, Donna.

Some people come into our lives and quickly go.
Others come and stay for a while
and leave "footprints" on our heart.
Somehow we are never quite the same.

~Author Unknown~

(I have this framed on the altar in my husband's mausoleum)

Friend's Comments

My Beloved's Funeral

It was too "beautiful" to be sad!
It was an "experience," not a funeral!
It was a "tribute" to a wonderful soul!

Remembering Frank

In the silence of summer you took your last breath. Your gentle passing was the answer to our prayers. A quiet closure for a gentle man. Gentleness was your strength, which we will always treasure.

We thank you for being in our lives! We are thankful for all you have "taught" us! You helped mold us into better individuals. You helped us grow! We shall always "cherish" your memory. We miss your lectures, but most of all we miss your smile!

A Simple Prayer

Lord make me an instrument of your peace
Where there is hatred ... let me sow love
Where there is injury ... pardon
Where there is discord ... unity
Where there is doubt ... faith
Where there is error ... truth
Where there is despair ... hope
Where there is sadness ... joy
Where there is darkness ... light
Oh Divine Master, grant that I may not so
much seek
To be consoled ... as to console
To be understood as to understand
To be loved ... as to love
For
It is in giving ... that we receive
It is in pardoning, that we are pardoned
It is in dying ... that we are born to eternal life

~St. Francis~

My husband and I traveled to Assisi, Italy twice. I traveled there again after his death. I buried his handkerchief in a church garden along with a tiny angel pin.

Farewell

Good bye to the life I used to live,
and the world I used to know
and kiss the hills for me just once
now I am ready to go!

~Emily Dickenson~
from her poem "farewell"

My Early Morning Message

I received upon awakening: You have been taught mastery! Your angels have taught you to master the acceptance of this illness. You have succeeded in helping with your loved one's gentle passage. Feel proud!

Hospice and Caregivers

H - Humble
O - Offering
S - Special
P - People
I - In
C - Common
E - Effort

I dedicate the above to "Danion Brinkley" and all hospice workers and caregivers everywhere!

Ending

Let your light so shine before men that they may see your good works.

~Matthew 5:16~
King James Version

I believe my husband's light did shine through his life's work and love of all people.

My beloved's wish was for world peace. Peace begins inside each and every one of us! To make a difference in this world, the difference has to begin with me, and with you! We must "feel" peace, "be" peace and "share" peace!

I only hope that my light will so shine through the words given me for this book that it lights your pathway. May it give you enough hope to lighten your load! Please understand, you "do" come out the other side! It is your "choice" as to whether you come out whole!

We all must understand grief is a "passage," not a place to stay!

Until we meet again, in person or on the printed page, I leave you in love and light.

Namaste!
JJ

Printed in the United States
By Bookmasters